ISBN 978-0-9838120-2-9

First published on 11/11/11 by Huqua Press
An Operating Division of Morling Manor Corporation
Los Angeles, California

Cover and text design by Alexandra Conn

HUQUA PRESS

huquapress.com

A portion of the proceeds from the sale of this book will be donated
to the End Hunger Network

Printed in the United States of America

The Supernatural Kids Cookbook
Super Special 11/11/11 Edition

by Nancy Mehagian

illustrations by Alexandra Conn

TABLE OF CONTENTS

The Supernatural Kids Cookbook

A good chef cooks from the heart.

INTRODUCTION

The date **11/11/11** is super SPECIAL because it will only happen once in our lifetime. Since so many junior chefs have been asking for even more Supernatural recipes, I decided to honor this unique day with eleven new ones. Some of these recipes are super easy and you'll want to make them all the time. And then there are some others that will *teach* you new skills.

COOKING is easy if you just follow the recipe and there's so much you can learn while you're in the kitchen. If your family is small and the recipe says it serves six you can use math to cut the recipe ingredients in half. If you come from a big family or you are having a PARTY you can always double the recipe.

The most important thing is to have fun while you're cooking. All of your happy thoughts and *good vibrations* go into the food along with the ingredients.

— Nancy Mehagian

BEFORE YOU BEGIN...

Wash your hands with soap and warm water. (Get off to a clean start!)

Have some kitchen towels handy and wear an *apron*.

Read each recipe all the way through and make sure you understand all the steps. Sometimes directions are also found in the list of ingredients. For example, a recipe may state: egg, slightly beaten. This means you should lightly beat the egg before adding it to the other ingredients. If the recipe calls for a cup of chopped onions and a cup of chopped potatoes, it's best to chop these vegetables before you do anything else and have all your ingredients ready at hand before you begin. If something seems confusing, *ask an adult* who knows their way around.

An *informed* Supernatural Chef
is a *smart* Supernatural Chef.

Get out all the **equipment** you need before you start to prepare each recipe. And if you learn to clean up as you go along, there won't be a big mess when you're done. Chances are you will be invited back to cook in the kitchen.

If necessary, be sure to preheat the oven.

And the most important thing of all—**SAFETY!** Be careful when using knives. Ask an adult to show you how to properly hold the knife when you are cutting vegetables. Of course, when you are baking or cooking on the stovetop use a potholder or kitchen mitt to avoid burns. Until you get to be an expert cook, it's better to have an adult supervising you.

KITCHEN EQUIPMENT

Kitchen Equipment

You might not need everything listed here because some items do double duty. If there is an electric mixer in your kitchen, then you can do without an eggbeater. Sometimes I'll use my electric blender instead of a whisk. If your oven comes with a timer, you won't need one of those either. Not everyone needs a *SALAD SPINNER* (used to get the water off the lettuce leaves you've just washed) but I can't live without mine since I eat salad every day. There are lots of fun and fancy cooking items and GADGETS on the market, but don't get carried away, otherwise you'll have drawers filled with things you rarely use.

Knives

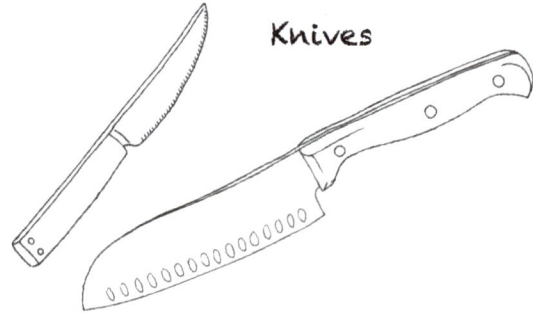

Juicer (for lemons, limes, etc.)

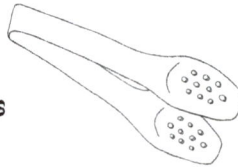

Tongs

Vegetable peeler

Measuring spoons

Potholders

Whisk

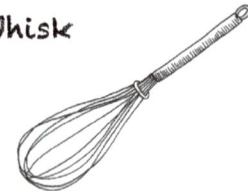

Other Kitchen Items:

- ➷ Apple corer
- ☾ Measuring cups
- ❀ Salad spinner
- ♭ Garlic press
- ❀ Electric mixer
- ∾ Mortar and Pestle
- ⚘ Electric blender

- ☾ Strainers
- ❀ Baking pans
- ❀ Muffin tins
- ♭ Timer
- ❀ Vegetable brush
- ❀ Skillets (my favorite skillet is made from cast iron and I have used it for years.)

Steamer basket

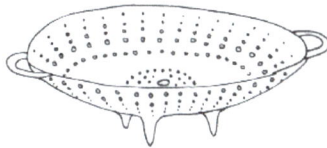

Mixing spoons

Spatula

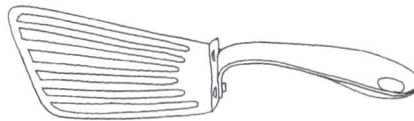

Grater

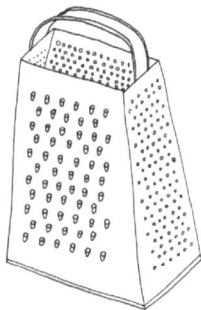

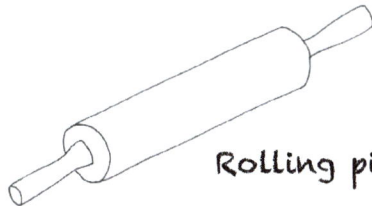

Rolling pin

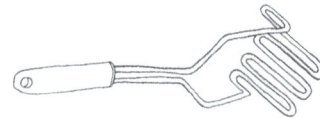

Potato masher

COOKING TERMS (YOU NEED TO KNOW)

Bake .... Cook in an oven

Beat .... Mix vigorously with a spoon, beater or in an electric mixer

Blend .... Combine two or more ingredients thoroughly

Boil .... Cook in a liquid so hot that it bubbles and keeps on bubbling

Chop .... Cut into pieces with a knife

Cream .... Stir until creamy

DICE .... Cut into very small squares (about ¼ inch)

DOT .... Drop bits of butter here and there over food

Drain .... Pour off liquid, often using a strainer

FLOUR .... Dust greased pan with flour until well covered on the bottom and sides

Fold .... Combine gently, in an over-and-under motion, until well blended

GREASE .... Spread bottom and sides of pan with butter, oil or cooking spray

KNEAD .... Work dough with the hands in a punching and pressing motion

MINCE .... Chop into very tiny pieces

Sauté .... To fry quickly in a little fat

Shred .... Slice as thin as you can, lengthwise

Sift .... Put flour through a sifter to remove lumps and bumps

Simmer .... Cook over very low heat

Toss .... Mix lightly

WHIP .... Add air by beating with an eggbeater or electric mixer

The Supernatural Kids Cookbook

TAMARI ROASTED PEPITAS

Pepitas is another name for **pumpkin seeds**. I don't know about you, but I love pumpkin seeds, especially when they are **crunchy** and have the sweet/salty flavor of soy sauce. Pepitas make a great **SNACK** and they are so good for us. Have you ever heard of manganese, magnesium, iron, zinc, phosphorus and copper? Those are all the **minerals** that are found in pumpkin seeds plus a good amount of protein and fiber.

Preheat oven to **350° F**

3 cups raw shelled pumpkin seeds
2 tablespoons olive oil
2 tablespoons Tamari soy sauce

In a bowl, **mix** the pumpkin seeds with olive oil and Tamari, using a wooden spoon to mix them well. Spread the seeds evenly on a baking sheet. Put them in the oven and **BAKE** for **12-14 minutes**. Halfway through, turn them over using your spatula so they get evenly baked. Remove from the oven when slightly browned. Allow them to **cool** and store them in a zip-lock bag.

BAKED PARMESAN ZUCCHINI STICKS

Preheat oven to **450° F**

Cooking spray
4 medium zucchini
¼ cup whole wheat flour
2 eggs, beaten
1 cup breadcrumbs

¼ cup grated Parmesan cheese
½ teaspoon dried oregano
¼ teaspoon garlic powder
½ teaspoon salt
¼ teaspoon black pepper

Begin by covering a baking sheet with cooking spray and set it aside. Then WASH and dry the zucchini and trim off the ends. Slice each zucchini down the middle then slice each half into thirds so they look like long, skinny sticks.

Arrange three bowls in a row. The first bowl is for the whole wheat flour. Bowl number two is for the beaten eggs and in bowl number three mix the breadcrumbs, Parmesan, oregano, garlic powder, salt and pepper. Now you have your zucchini assembly line.

Dip the zucchini sticks in the flour, then the egg and finally the breadcrumb mixture. Try to coat them well. Lay them on the cookie sheet. When all the zucchini have been breaded, *bake* them for **10 minutes.** Carefully turn them over with a spatula and bake them for another **10 minutes.** (Remember, the oven will be hot!) Serve them hot from the oven.

BUTTERNUT SQUASH & APPLE SOUP

Creamy (without the cream) and smooth and a definite winner in the soup category. It is not easy to cut the squash since it's quite hard and requires a good knife, so definitely ask for help cutting up the squash.

2 tablespoons butter
1 tablespoon olive oil
1 medium onion, chopped
2 celery stalks, sliced
1 medium-size butternut squash (approx. 4 cups)
2 organic Granny Smith apples, peeled, cored and chopped

4 cups chicken or vegetable broth
½ teaspoon garlic powder
½ teaspoon nutmeg
1 teaspoon salt
¼ teaspoon black pepper
Sour cream or plain Greek yogurt (optional)

Have an adult **help** you peel the butternut squash, remove the seeds from the inside then chop into chunk size pieces.

Melt butter in a large stockpot and add the olive oil. Sauté the onion and celery over medium heat for 5 minutes or until they soften.

Next add the squash, apple and broth and bring to a boil. Stir in the garlic powder, nutmeg, salt and pepper. Cover the pot with a lid, lower the heat to simmer and cook for **30 minutes** or until the squash and apple are soft enough to break up with a spoon. Remove the pot from the stove and let it cool a bit.

Carefully pour half of the soup into the jar of your blender and puree until smooth. Put soup into a clean pot. Then purée the other half. Serve the soup with a dollop of sour cream or plain Greek yogurt on top.

🌿 Serves 6

7

SEDONA TORTILLA SOUP

I was born and raised in the Southwest so I love a good tortilla soup. Every time I make this people come back for more. This is something your entire family will love. Around my house we keep the Tabasco sauce handy for people who like their tortilla soup really SPICY.

1 pound boneless, skinless chicken breast tenders
1 tablespoon cumin
1 tablespoon chile powder
2 tablespoons olive oil
1 large red onion, chopped
½ red bell pepper, chopped
2 or 3 cloves garlic, minced
1 teaspoon oregano
1 cup tomato sauce
6 cups of chicken broth
1 ½ teaspoons salt
½ teaspoon black pepper
Juice of 2 or 3 limes
½ cup chopped fresh cilantro
6 corn tortillas, sliced into strips
1 cup crumbled Cotija cheese,
Queso Fresco or your favorite grated Cheddar

Start by *cutting* the chicken in strips. I like to use my kitchen scissors for this. (When working with raw chicken it's important to **wash** your hands with warm water and soap after handling it as well as washing the cutting board.) Put the spices, the cumin and chile powder, into a bowl, mix and then toss the chicken in the spice mixture and rub them around until the pieces are all well *coated*.

Next heat the olive oil in a stockpot and **sauté** the chicken in it for about **5 minutes**. Then stir in the onion, bell pepper and garlic and continue sautéing for about **10 minutes more**, until the onions and pepper are soft. Add the oregano, tomato sauce, chicken broth, salt and pepper and let the mixture come to a full boil. Then lower the heat to **simmer**, cover with a lid and cook for **30 minutes**.

Finally, stir in the lime juice, the chopped cilantro and the corn tortillas. Cook for a **few minutes more**, until the tortillas *FALL* apart and thicken the soup. Serve with the crumbled or grated cheese on top. **OLE!**

❧ **Serves 6**

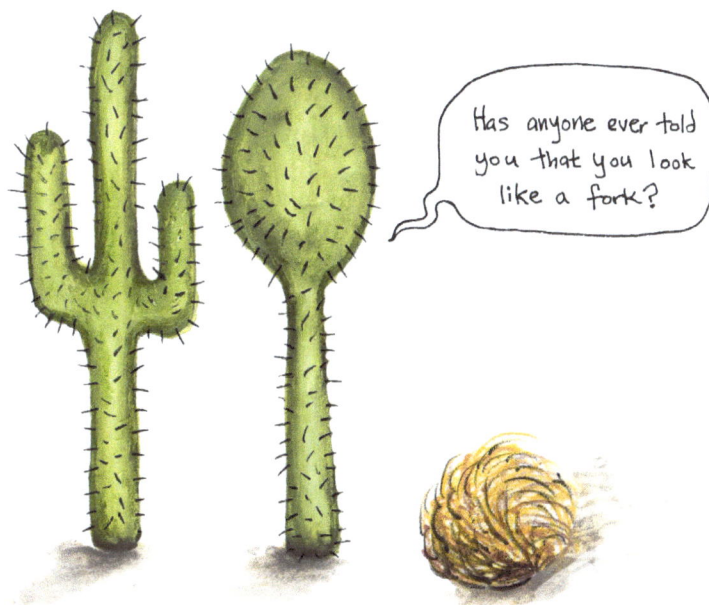

9

BBQ TURKEY MEATBALLS

Turkey meatballs are fun to make and so tasty to eat. Without the BBQ sauce you could even put them into the spaghetti sauce I hope you learned to make in the first Supernatural Kids Cookbook. Or you could just eat them with brown rice and a salad.

Preheat oven to **375° F**

1 lb. ground turkey
1 small onion, chopped fine
½ medium zucchini, grated (about ½ cup)
1 egg, beaten
½ cup whole wheat bread crumbs
1 teaspoon salt

¼ teaspoon black pepper
¼ teaspoon garlic powder
½ teaspoon thyme
½ teaspoon rubbed sage
½ cup of your favorite natural BBQ sauce

In a mixing bowl, blend all the ingredients except the BBQ sauce together and mix well. You can use your hands or a spoon. Then form balls by ROLLING the mixture between your palms and place the meatballs in an 8-inch square-baking dish. Pour the BBQ sauce on top of them and bake in the oven for **45 minutes.**

WHOLE WHEAT CHEDDAR BISCUITS

Preheat oven to **400° F**

> 2 cups whole wheat flour
> 2 tablespoons baking powder
> ½ teaspoon baking soda
> 1 tablespoon raw sugar
> ½ teaspoon salt
> 4 tablespoons cold butter
> ¾ cup buttermilk
> ¾ cup finely grated sharp Cheddar cheese

In a large mixing bowl, combine the flour, baking powder, baking soda, sugar and salt. Using a pastry blender **CUT** in the butter and until the mixture looks **crumbly**. Next add in the buttermilk and the cheese and stir just until the dry ingredients are wet. It's important not to over mix. Use an ice cream scoop to **drop** golf ball-sized balls of dough onto an ungreased baking sheet. **Bake** for **12-15 minutes** or until the tops of the biscuits turn light brown.

🐝 **Makes 12 biscuits**

VEDRA'S PASTA SALAD

I named this pasta salad for my daughter since it was her *favorite* school lunch. I made it a little different every time and all her friends would always ask for a bite. Sometimes I would make it with turkey, sometimes I would add some asparagus. Once in a while I would roast the peppers and occasionally I'd add *chopped* olives. That's what is so much fun about making it. You can use your own **ideas** to make it special. For those **Supernatural Kids** who can't eat gluten, now there is every kind of pasta available at your local health food market. Feel free to substitute as needed.

1 pound whole wheat penne pasta	Dressing:
1 cup frozen peas, cooked	2 tablespoons olive oil
2 cups steamed broccoli florets	2 tablespoons red wine vinegar
2 large ripe tomatoes chopped (about 2 cups)	¼ teaspoon garlic powder
½ red bell pepper, diced	Salt and pepper to taste
⅓ cup chopped fresh basil	
1 cup grated Parmesan cheese	

Cook the pasta according to the directions on the package. **Drain** pasta and put it in a bowl. Then add the peas, broccoli, tomatoes, bell pepper, basil and Parmesan.

Mix the dressing in a small bowl or shake it in a jar. **Pour** the dressing over the top, give the salad a good toss with a wooden spoon and serve it room temperature. It makes a great light Sunday supper and is perfect for your lunch box the next day.

🌱 Serves 6

APPLE BUCKLE

A buckle is a variation of a cobbler and it is a traditional American dish. It was often eaten for breakfast by the early colonists using whatever fresh fruit or *berries* were in season. With the fruit on the top it has a "buckled" appearance when it is **baked**.

Preheat oven to **325° F**

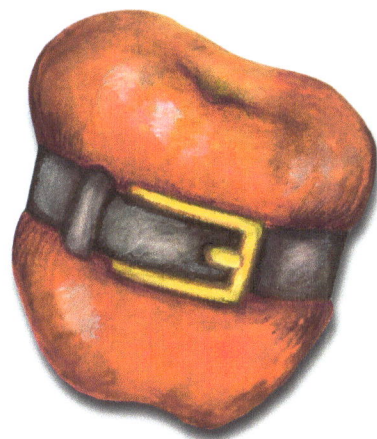

¾ **cup butter, room temperature**

1 **cup** raw sugar

2 **eggs**

1 **teaspoon** vanilla

1 **tablespoon grated** lemon zest

1 ½ **cups** white whole wheat flour

1 **teaspoon** baking powder

¼ **teaspoon** salt

¼ **teaspoon** nutmeg

⅓ **cup** milk **(low-fat is fine)**

3 **organic** Granny Smith apples**, peeled and sliced**

2 **tablespoons** brown sugar

1 **teaspoon** cinnamon

GREASE an 8-inch square baking pan with butter and then dust with flour and set aside.
In the bowl of your electric mixer *CREAM* the butter and sugar together until smooth, at least 3 minutes. Stir in the eggs, one at a time, and continue beating. Then add the vanilla and lemon zest.

In another bowl, **mix** the dry ingredients (flour, baking powder, salt and nutmeg) together. Slowly blend in half of flour mixture into the butter mixture. Add the milk and finally the remaining flour mixture and mix until a smooth batter is formed.

Scrape the batter into the baking pan and then lay the apple slices on top. If you do this **neatly** your cake will look better. *Sprinkle* the apples with the brown sugar and cinnamon and bake in the oven for **60 minutes**, or until a knife inserted into the center comes out clean

PUMPKIN BUNDT CAKE WITH WHITE CHOCOLATE & PECANS

This is one delicious cake—moist, spicy and sure to please everyone. It's made with canned pumpkin so you don't have to wait until the holidays to make it. It's a little known fact that there is more beta-carotene (a very important nutrient) in pumpkin when it is cooked. Like many orange vegetables, pumpkin is loaded with vitamins and minerals as well as fiber. You can give a SPOON of it to your dogs too since it's also really good for them.

The hardest part of this recipe is GREASING and flouring the bundt pan but once you get the hang of it you'll be able to do it in no time at all.

Preheat oven to **350° F**

3 cups whole wheat flour or white whole wheat flour

2 teaspoons baking powder

2 teaspoons baking soda

3 teaspoons cinnamon

1 teaspoon salt

4 eggs, beaten

2 cups raw sugar

1 ¼ cups canola oil

1 teaspoon vanilla extract

One 15 ounce can of pumpkin
(approx. 2 cups cooked, mashed pumpkin)

1 cup white chocolate chips

½ cup chopped pecans or walnuts

BUTTER and flour a bundt pan. Use a little bit of paper towel and soft butter to do the job and try not to miss anything on the sides or in the middle of the pan.

The next step is to put a little flour in the pan and kind of *swoosh* it around until there is a dusting of flour everywhere. Like the butter, you don't want to miss a spot with the flour. Giving the pan a hard SHAKE will loosen all the excess flour so you can dump that bit out. (It should only be a little because we don't want to waste anything we don't have to). Set the pan aside.

Sift all the dry ingredients together into a big bowl. I put everything through the sifter—the flour, baking powder and soda, spices and salt. Mix with a wooden spoon and set aside.

In another bowl or in your mixer, **beat** the eggs and sugar together until they look light and creamy. Add the oil and pumpkin and continue beating at medium speed. Now slowly stir in the flour mixture, a bit at a time. Finally FOLD in the chips and the nuts.

POUR the batter into the bundt pan and bake in the oven for **60 minutes.** I use a long skewer (kind of like an extra long toothpick) to test the cake to make sure it's done. Let the cake sit for at least **30 minutes** before you turn it upside down onto a cake platter. Bundt pans are heavy so you might need some help doing this the first time.

Wait about half an hour more before you dig into your masterpiece.

SUGAR & SPICE COOKIES

I predict these EASY-TO-MAKE cookies will become one of your favorites. The recipe calls for MOLASSES, a sweetener that is actually good for you. It's made from processing sugar cane and contains good amounts of minerals, especially iron. If you spray a little cooking spray in the measuring cup before you measure the molasses it will pour easily.

Preheat oven to **350° F**

¾ cup butter, softened to room temperature	1 tablespoon ground ginger
1 cup raw sugar	1 teaspoon cinnamon
⅓ cup molasses	1 teaspoon baking soda
1 egg	¼ teaspoon salt
2 ½ cups white whole wheat flour	

Begin by covering 2 baking sheets with aluminum foil, then set them aside. In a mixing bowl or the bowl of your mixer cream the butter and ¾ cup of the sugar together for 3 minutes. Stir in the molasses and continue beating. Next add the egg and continue beating.

In another bowl mix the flour, ginger, cinnamon, baking soda and salt together. Slowly add the flour mixture to the wet mixture and mix just until everything is blended and a soft dough is formed.

Put the remaining ¼ cup of sugar into a small bowl. SHAPE the dough into 1-inch balls by rolling gently in the palm of your hand. Then roll each ball in the sugar and place on the foil-covered baking sheet, making sure to leave about 1 inch between them. (Cookies will spread out when they are baking.) Bake them for **10-13 minutes**.

Makes about **3 dozen cookies**

BAKED BANANAS

Baked bananas are my favorite *easy* dessert. You have to try them to know how delicious they are. They can be served with yogurt, whipped cream, a scoop of vanilla ice cream or just on their own. If you like bananas, you will love them baked.

¼ cup (½ stick) melted butter (I use my microwave to melt the butter.)
1 teaspoon grated lemon zest
3 tablespoons lemon juice
5 firm ripe bananas
5 tablespoons brown sugar

Pour melted butter into a baking dish (8-inch square). Add the lemon zest and lemon juice and stir to blend. **Peel** the bananas and line them up in the baking dish, turning them over so all of the bananas are coated with the butter mixture. *Sprinkle* brown sugar on top and place in the oven for **10 minutes.** Remove the pan and carefully turn over each banana. Then return the pan to the oven and bake for **10 minutes more.**

That's it! ENJOY!

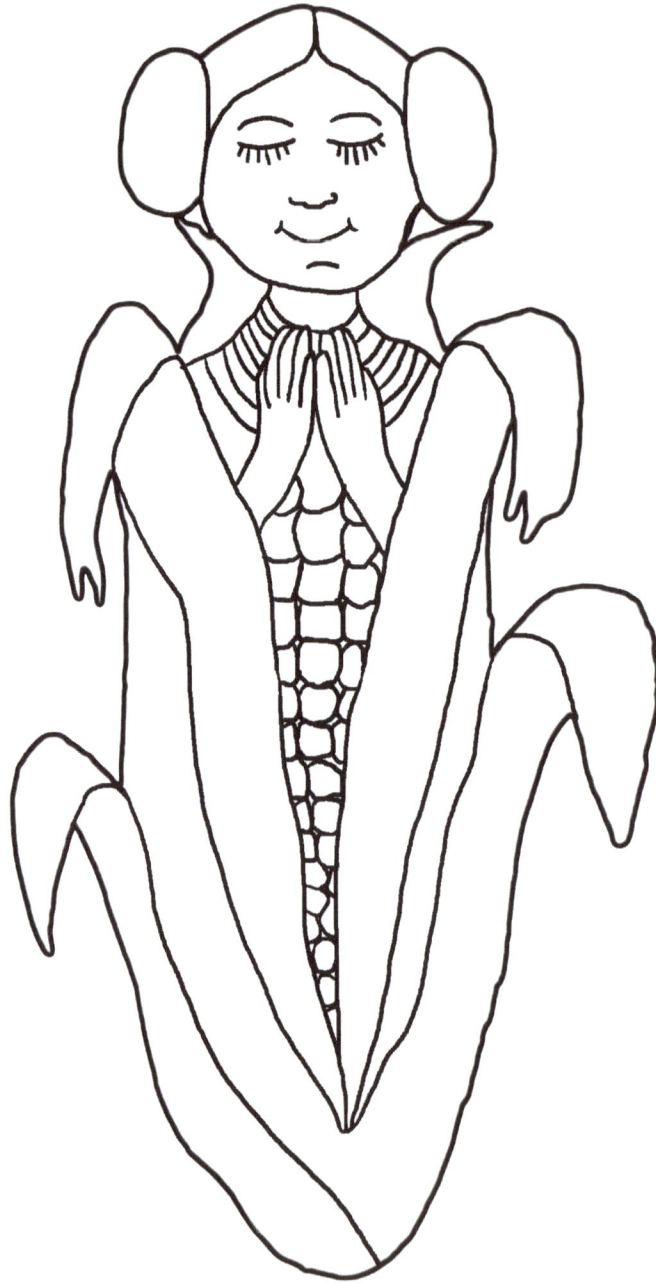

19

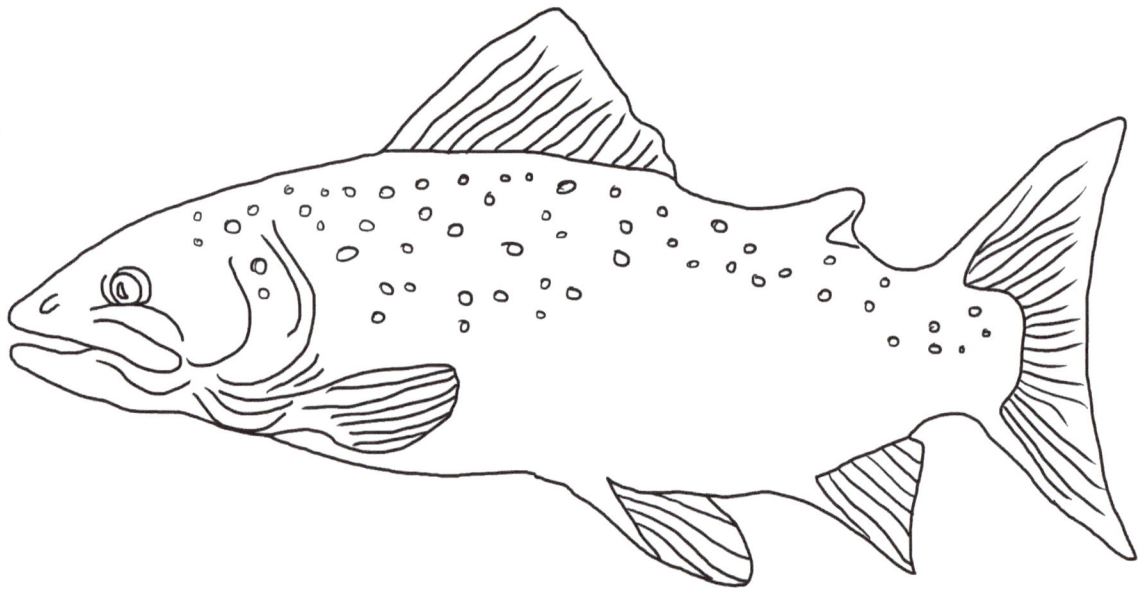

ACKNOWLEDGEMENTS

Without my dream team of Judy Proffer and Alexandra Conn, Supernatural Kids Cookbook might still be caught in a time warp. I feel like the luckiest person to be able to work with such smart, talented and creative women. A big shout out to Spencer Proffer whose support and enthusiasm knows no bounds and in my book qualifies as Super Mensch.

And last, but never least I owe so much to my long-time friend Coco Conn who I have counted on for as long as I can remember for her brilliance and knowledge.

www.ingramcontent.com/pod-product-compliance
Lightning Source LLC
Chambersburg PA
CBHW061158030426
42337CB00002B/38